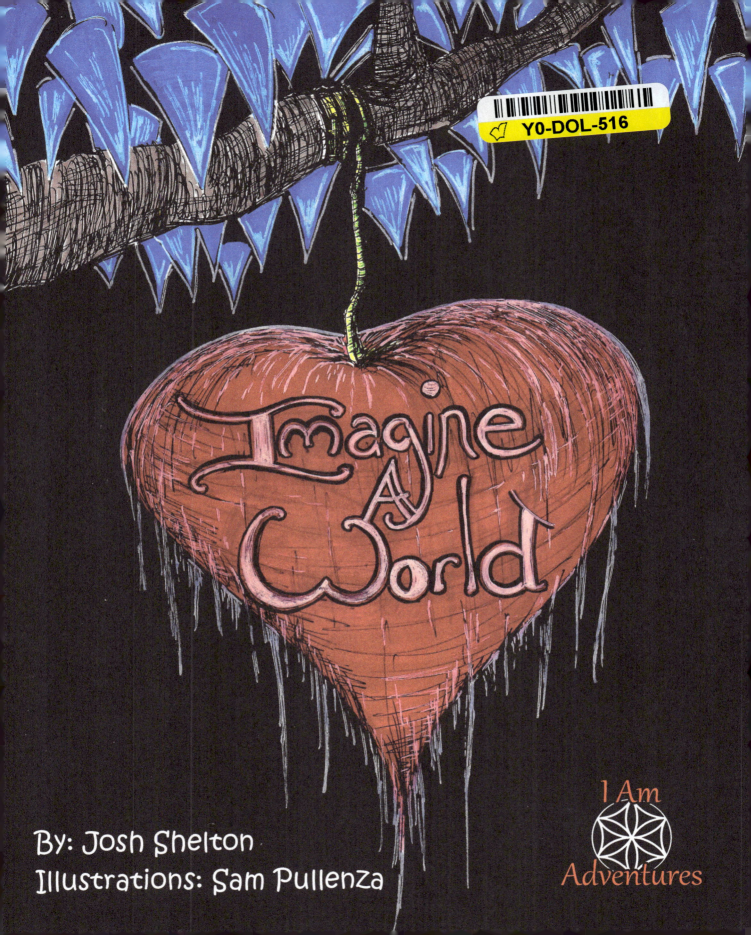

Imagine A World

By: Josh Shelton
Illustrations: Sam Pullenza

I Am
Adventures

First Printed in United Kingdom 2019
Published by Conscious Dreams Publishing
www.consciousdreamspublishing.com

Designed by Josh Shelton and Sam Pullenza
www.whitemagicbooks.net

Illustrated by Sam Pullenza

Edited by Rhoda Molife
www.molahmedia.com

ISBN: 978-1-912551-74-3

This book is dedicated to Amanda.
Within all of the worlds I have ever imagined,
I've found you dancing to the sound of silence,
forever young, beautiful, and free.

And to the ascension of Planet Earth
and all who call her home.

Won't you please join our tribe?

We're embarking

On a most magnificent ride !!!

She's rising from slumber

To the shine of the sun

A great awakening is dawning

It's already begun

For this change to take flight
It must come from within!

So strap up your light boots

Unbuckle your heart

Free your mind...

It's 'create-with-our-imagination-time!'

With fresh water abound...

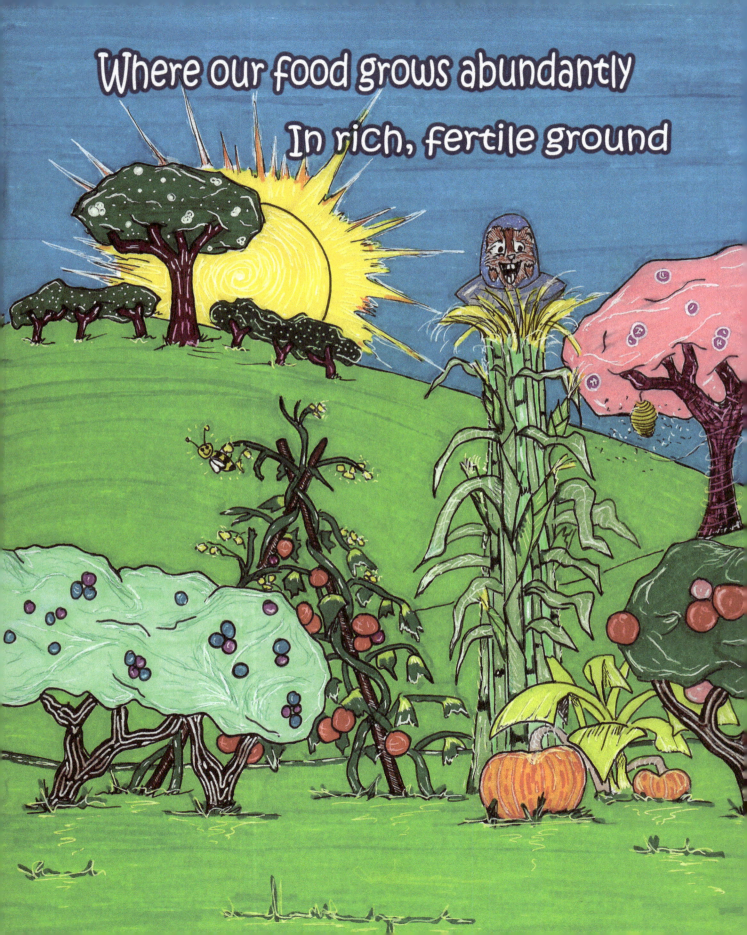

Imagine all beings

Warm and fed

Where every soul has a soft place

To rest their head

Dream

Imagine a world
Where we reveal the secrets
Of our past...

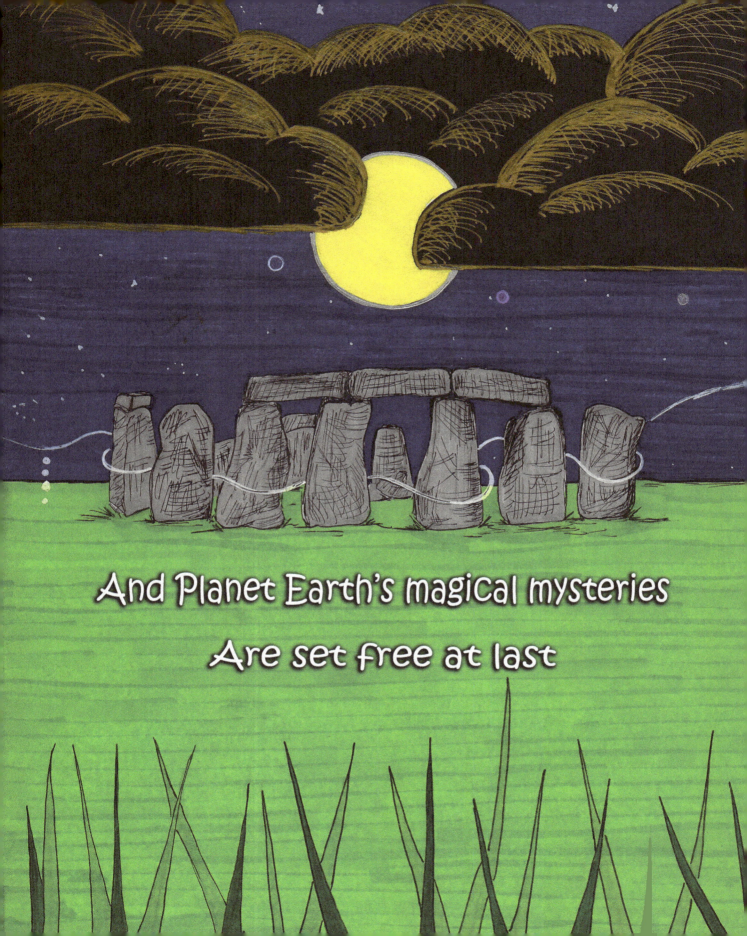

And Planet Earth's magical mysteries

Are set free at last

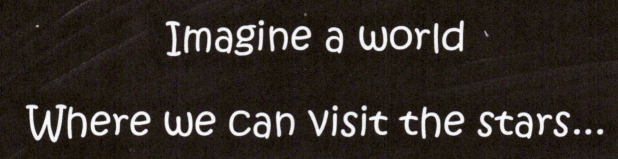

Imagine a world

Where we can visit the stars...

Play tag on the moon
And hopscotch on Mars

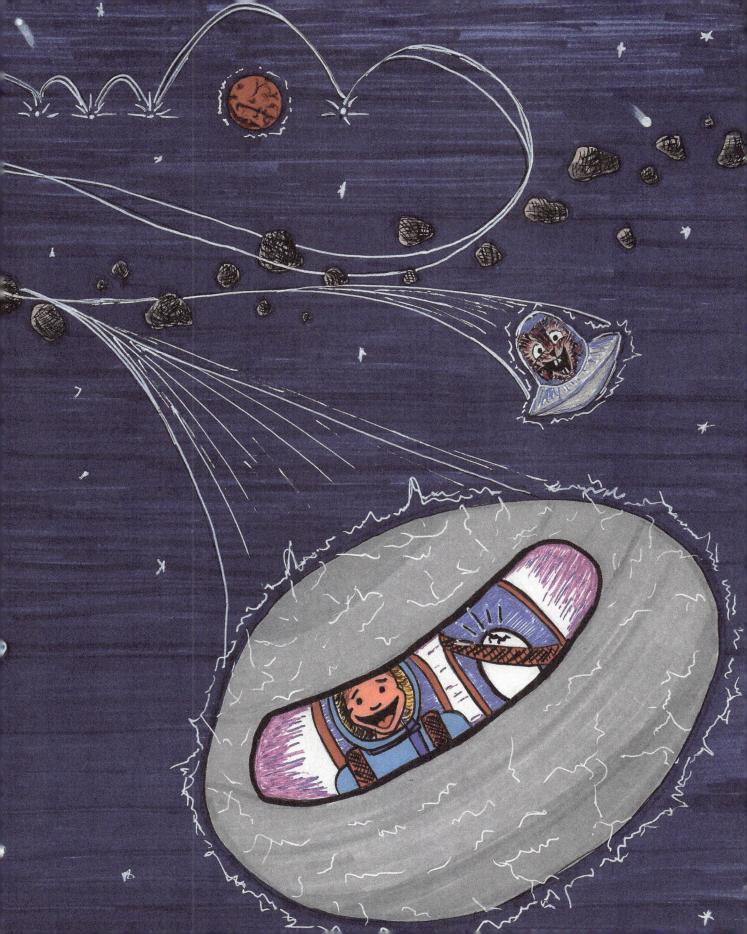

Imagine a world
Where real healing takes place
And freedom engulfs
The whole human race

We've traveled so far
But we're not done just yet

With our feet on the ground
Let's pause and reflect...

Can you imagine a world

Where united as one we all stand?

And LOVE

Will be the only law of the land?

YES I CAN
!!!

I imagine a world
Where I love all I see

And all I see loves me back
When it looks at me

But if you go deep within
We're all the same
Oh yes, indeed!

You may be gigantic and hairy

Have wings like a fairy

Or the ears

Of a small garden gnome

But whatever your shape

Color or Size

We all share Planet Earth

As our home

She is asking us
To answer her call
Because...

Where we go one
Is where we go all

The moment is

NOW

The time to wait
Is no more
We are the ones
We've been waiting for

I imagine this world
Yet deep down within
I can remember this world
And I will create it again

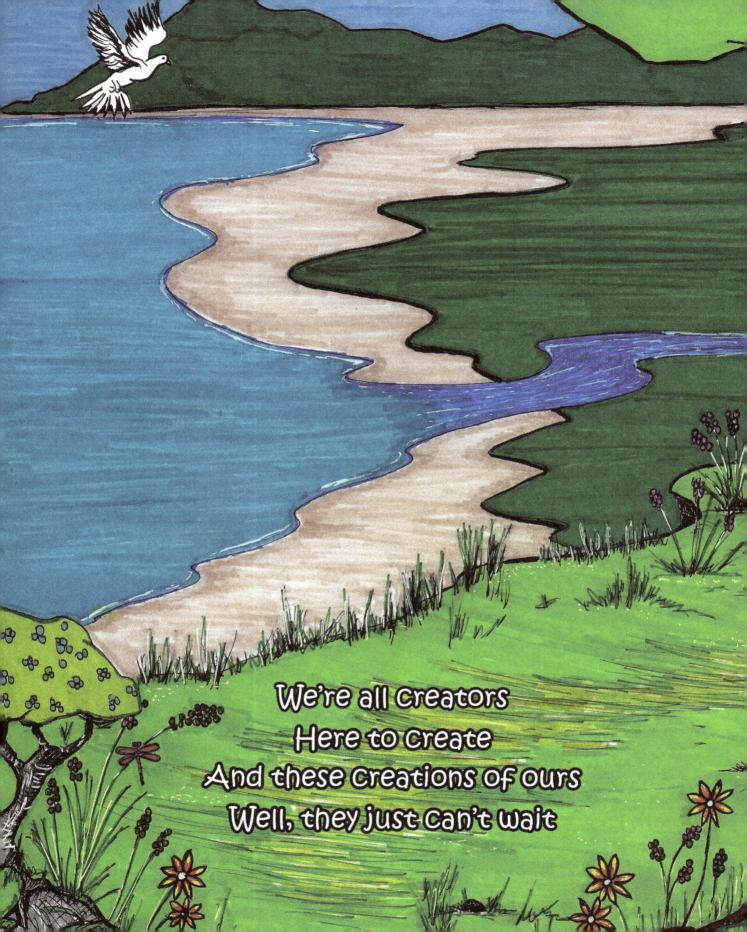

We're all creators
Here to create
And these creations of ours
Well, they just can't wait

So from the tip-tops of our mountains
To the deepest depths of our seas
We have imagined this world...

And
SO it will BE!!!

Please visit

WhiteMagicBooks.net

for more

'I Am'

Adventures!

Conscious Dreams
PUBLISHING

Be the author of your own destiny

Find out about our authors, events, services
and how you too can get your book journey started.

- Conscious Dreams Publishing
- @DreamsConscious
- @consciousdreamspublishing
- Daniella Blechner
- www.consciousdreamspublishing.com
- info@consciousdreamspublishing.com

Let's connect

CPSIA information can be obtained
at www.ICGtesting.com
Printed in the USA
JSHW021928291019
2153JS00001B/3